Discover the
Rewards of
Authentic
Relationships

THE
REAL DEAL

Interactions Small Group Series

Authenticity: Being Honest with God and Others
Character: Reclaiming Six Endangered Qualities
Commitment: Developing Deeper Devotion to Christ
Community: Building Relationships within God's Family
Essential Christianity: Practical Steps for Spiritual Growth
Fruit of the Spirit: Living the Supernatural Life
Getting a Grip: Finding Balance in Your Daily Life
Jesus: Seeing Him More Clearly
Lessons on Love: Building Deeper Relationships
Living in God's Power: Finding God's Strength for Life's Challenges
Love in Action: Experiencing the Joy of Serving
Marriage: Building Real Intimacy
Meeting God: Psalms for the Highs and Lows of Life
New Identity: Discovering Who You Are in Christ
Parenting: How to Raise Spiritually Healthy Kids
Prayer: Opening Your Heart to God
Reaching Out: Sharing God's Love Naturally
The Real Deal: Discover the Rewards of Authentic Relationships
Significance: Understanding God's Purpose for Your Life
Transformation: Letting God Change You from the Inside Out

InterActions
small group series

Discover the
Rewards of
Authentic
Relationships

THE
REAL DEAL

Previously published as *Transparency*

BILL HYBELS
WITH KEVIN AND SHERRY HARNEY

ZONDERVAN™

GRAND RAPIDS, MICHIGAN 49530 USA

WILLOW
Willow Creek Resources

ZONDERVAN™

The Real Deal
Copyright © 1997 by Willow Creek Association
Previously published as *Transparency*

Requests for information should be addressed to:

Zondervan, *Grand Rapids, Michigan 49530*

ISBN-10: 0-310-26601-7
ISBN-13: 978-0-310-26601-3

Interior design by Rick Devon and Michelle Espinoza

Printed in the United States of America

---

05 06 07 08 09 10 11 12 /❖ DCI/ 10 9 8 7 6 5 4 3 2 1

CONTENTS

INTERACTIONS

In 1992, Willow Creek Community Church, in partnership with Zondervan and the Willow Creek Association, released a curriculum for small groups entitled the Walking with God series. In just three years, almost a half million copies of these small group study guides were being used in churches around the world. The phenomenal response to this curriculum affirmed the need for relevant and biblical small group materials.

At the writing of this curriculum, there are nearly 3,000 small groups meeting regularly within the structure of Willow Creek Community Church. We believe this number will increase as we continue to place a central value on small groups. Many other churches throughout the world are growing in their commitment to small group ministries as well, so the need for resources is increasing.

In response to this great need, the Interactions small group series has been developed. Willow Creek Association and Zondervan have joined together to create a whole new approach to small group materials. These discussion guides are meant to challenge group members to a deeper level of sharing, to create lines of accountability, to move followers of Christ into action, and to help group members become fully devoted followers of Christ.

SUGGESTIONS FOR INDIVIDUAL STUDY

1. Begin each session with prayer. Ask God to help you understand the passage and to apply it to your life.
2. A good modern translation, such as the New International Version, the New American Standard Bible, or the New Revised Standard Version, will give you the most help. Questions in this guide are based on the New International Version.
3. Read and reread the passage(s). You must know what the passage says before you can understand what it means and how it applies to you.
4. Write your answers in the spaces provided in the study guide. This will help you to express clearly your understanding of the passage.
5. Keep a Bible dictionary handy. Use it to look up unfamiliar words, names, or places.

Suggestions for Group Study

1. Come to the session prepared. Careful preparation will greatly enrich your time in group discussion.
2. Be willing to join in the discussion. The leader of the group will not be lecturing, but will encourage people to discuss what they have learned in the passage. Plan to share what God has taught you in your individual study.
3. Stick to the passage being studied. Base your answers on the verses being discussed rather than on outside authorities such as commentaries or your favorite author or speaker.
4. Try to be sensitive to the other members of the group. Listen attentively when they speak, and be affirming whenever you can. This will encourage more hesitant members of the group to participate.
5. Be careful not to dominate the discussion. By all means participate! But allow others to have equal time.
6. If you are the discussion leader, you will find additional suggestions and helpful ideas in the Leader's Notes.

Additional Resources and Teaching Materials

At the end of this study guide you will find a collection of resources and teaching materials to help you in your growth as a follower of Christ. You will also find resources that will help your church develop and build fully devoted followers of Christ.

Introduction: Discovering the Rewards of Authentic Relationships

If I told my boss the truth, he'd blow his stack.

If I told my husband what his constant traveling is doing to our family, he would get defensive.

If I told my parents how frustrated I am in school, they wouldn't understand.

If I told my wife about some of the sexual frustrations I feel in our relationship, she'd accuse me of having a one-track mind.

If I told my professor the real reason I didn't finish my paper on time, she'd dock my grade.

If I told my minister what I really thought about his sermons, he'd be crushed and discouraged.

On and on we go, giving reason after reason why we just can't afford to tell the truth. Most of us could write a book entitled *101 Good Reasons to Not Tell the Truth.* The sad fact is that truth-telling has fallen on hard times.

I'm sure even the most hardened cynic wouldn't want to debate the position the Bible takes on the subject of telling the truth. From cover to cover the Bible says, "Speak the truth in love." Number nine of the Ten Commandments says, "Don't give false testimony against your neighbor." Ephesians 4:25 addresses the absolutely critical nature of truth-telling: "Therefore each of you must put off falsehood and speak truthfully to his neighbor." Proverbs 8:7 says, " My mouth speaks what is true, for my lips detest wickedness." Few thinking people in our society—Christian or non-Christian— would deny that, in theory, honesty is the best policy.

But the hard reality is that, in the pressure of real-life relationships, truth does not always come out of our mouths. Too often our natural tendency is to do everything we can to "keep the peace." Sometimes this means refraining from telling the truth because of the chaos and tension it will bring into our lives and relationships. Other times, we feel the desire to be truthful, but we have a sense that the truth will not be received very well. In those moments, we often decide that truth-telling is a great idea . . . *for someone else.*

Sadly, many of us are in a relationship with a husband, wife, son, daughter, parent, friend, employer, employee, or someone else who has no idea we are covering up our true feelings. When we do this, we are making a calculated decision *not* to tell the truth about these matters because we attach a higher value on keeping the peace than on authentic relationships. But over time, this approach to relationships proves to be a costly error in judgment.

Our dilemma is that we all have inner yearnings to be in a significant relationship with someone with whom we can be completely honest and vulnerable. We all hunger for a person with whom we can share failures as well as successes, shortcomings as well as victories, our doubts and deepest fears. We all seek for that someone who will also relate to us with integrity, confidentiality, and love. We all yearn to have communal relationships.

Sadly, most of us seem to be stuck in pseudocommunal relationships. Pseudocommunal relationships are those that have the pretense and appearance of community, but in which real community doesn't exist. People in pseudocommunal relationships talk about safe subjects, carefully edit their conversations so as not to disclose the really private parts of their heart, and make sure to avoid all potential tension or chaos. In short, we sacrifice truth-telling on the altar of peacekeeping and never enter into real community.

This series of small group interactions will challenge you to levels of transparency that go beyond your relational comfort zone. You matter to God, and so do the people He has brought into your life. God longs for you to experience true community in your relationships. This means you will need to learn how to tell the truth to yourself, as well as to others. It also means you will need to commit yourself to telling the truth even if this means sacrificing the peace. But in doing so, what you will discover is God's true plan for human relationships . . . real community, real intimacy, and real transparency.

Bill Hybels

SECRET CONVERSATIONS

THE BIG PICTURE

Some years ago it was discovered that the new American embassy in Moscow was so loaded with electronic listening devices that every single conversation in the place could be picked up and recorded by the Russians, giving them instant access to private conversations. In fact, one report said that the entire steel structure of the building was like a giant antenna. Our governmental leaders were outraged, and rightly so.

A breach in confidentiality in foreign relations can be dangerous and costly. Private conversations are meant to be just that . . . private! When privacy is invaded, something is very wrong. When confidentiality is betrayed, sparks begin to fly! No one wants their private conversations made public.

We are all aware that private conversations go on between people, but did you know there are private conversations going on inside of you? We all talk to ourselves and carry on private conversations in our minds. These secret conversations we have with ourselves can be damaging or strengthening. One thing is for sure, it's probably a good thing there aren't electronic listening devices that can record and play back the private conversations that run through our mind each day.

A WIDE ANGLE VIEW

1 Describe how you felt when someone in your life took a private conversation you had with them and made it public information.

What impact did this have on your relationship?

A BIBLICAL PORTRAIT

Read John 8:31–32, 42–47

2 Describe the vivid and contrasting portraits of Jesus and Satan in this passage.

3 How does Jesus challenge the belief system of the religious leaders of His day?

How can these challenges speak to "religious" people today?

SHARPENING THE FOCUS

Read Snapshot "Secret Conversations About Your Self-Worth"

SECRET CONVERSATIONS ABOUT YOUR SELF-WORTH

Your secret conversations about your own worth or value are enormously important. If we could put an electronic listening device on some people, we might hear something like, "Everybody looks so normal and happy. What's the matter with me? Why don't I feel happy? Why can't I be more relaxed and secure? It's because I'm not attractive, bright, and witty like everyone else. And I'm certainly not as spiritual. Face it, I don't measure up. I really don't matter at all."

Many conversations like this happen in the minds of people throughout the day. In fact, some people experience steady streams of self-talk that denigrate their self-worth day after day, week after week, month after month, year after year. These conversations are not benign banterings; rather like a deadly cancer, they take a dreadful toll.

Contrast the above conversation with the private conversation going on in someone else's mind: "I live my day among countless people and yet the God of the Universe is thinking of me each moment. He knows my name. The hairs of my head are numbered. He enjoys my fellowship, prayers, and worship. He delights in me as I walk with Him. I can feel His smile as I seek to follow Him each day." Can you hear the difference? One conversation ends in defeat and discouragement, the other in praise and celebration. When we think about it this way, it's easy to see how our secret conversations about our self-worth have a powerful impact on our lives.

4 Most of us have secret conversations about our self-worth that cover both sides of the above spectrum. If your fellow small group members could hear your secret conversations about your self-worth, what is one thing they would learn about you?

5 When you have positive secret conversations about your own self-worth, what are the sources of this positive view of yourself?

Read Snapshot "Secret Conversations About Personal Competency"

SECRET CONVERSATIONS ABOUT PERSONAL COMPETENCY

We need to be very sensitive about our private conversations when it comes to the area of personal competency. Imagine two people driving to their first day of a new job. One is in the car saying to himself, "This is going to be a disaster. I'm in way over my head. I'm going to wind up blowing this thing. I never do anything well. I make stupid mistakes. I wonder how long this job will last? Probably as long as my last one."

A woman is a mile back on the same expressway holding her own private conversation. She's saying, "You know, first days are always awkward. But that's life. The awkwardness will pass. It always does. I can probably learn the ropes with a little time, and all I have to do is give it my best shot. I'll probably do just fine, especially with help from above. I'm going to trust You today, Lord, and I know that You never fail."

Which of these two people has a better chance of succeeding? When it comes to personal competency matters, self-talk is critical!

---

6 Choose *one* of the areas listed below and give an example of what a negative secret conversation about personal competency might sound like:

- Going out on a first date
- Starting a small business
- Being asked to serve in a church ministry
- Going back to school for additional education

What can you do to fight against the natural tendency to have these kinds of debilitating negative secret conversations?

7

Using the same area you chose above, give an example of what a *positive* secret conversation about personal competency might sound like.

What can you do to develop a more positive internal dialogue about your personal competency?

Read Snapshot "Secret Conversations About Spiritual Matters"

SECRET CONVERSATIONS ABOUT SPIRITUAL MATTERS

As in personal matters, self-talk can also flow freely, and often unconsciously, in the area of spiritual matters. The importance of spiritual self-talk cannot be overemphasized. The quality of your life—and perhaps your eternal destiny—hinges upon your private spiritual conversations and the subsequent conclusions you come to in those internal dialogues.

Some people talk to themselves with real honesty. They say, "I know I have sinned against God and have made a mess of my life. I also know I am lost without a Savior to make things right between me and God." These people cry out, "Jesus, thank You for giving Your whole life for me. You have offered me a new beginning and forgiveness for all my sins. Without You I am lost, and because of You I have been found." This is the most important private conversation we can ever have.

Others fight the truth and continue to tell themselves lies. They say, "There is no God. There is no heaven or hell. I won't ever be judged for the life I have lived and the decisions I have made." Sometimes they even try to comfort themselves by saying, "If there is a God and a heaven, I'm sure things will work out in the end. I've been a pretty good person." These private conversations can be more costly than most people ever dream. They are secret lies which keep people from recognizing their need for a Savior.

8 If you have come to the point where you have told the truth to God and acknowledged your need of His saving power in your life, how has this spiritual truth-telling transformed your life?

9 If you have not come to the point where you have admitted to God that you need a Savior, what is standing in the way?

PUTTING YOURSELF IN THE PICTURE

Four-Step Process

1. Take time to reflect on the thoughts that pass through your mind in the course of a day. Try to become keenly aware of any private conversations you are having.
2. Make sure everything you are saying to yourself is truthful, no matter how much it hurts or how uncomfortable or exposed you feel. Evaluate your private conversations about self-worth, personal competency, and spiritual matters.
3. Locate any lie that finds its way into your internal dialogues. Then label it as a lie! A lie cannot be tolerated. It needs to be exposed.
4. Once the lie is exposed and labeled for what it is, it needs to be renounced and replaced with the truth of God. Study the Bible to discover God's truth. If you need help in a specific area, ask another follower of Christ to help you discover God's truth in this area of your life.

THE TRUTH WILL SET YOU FREE!

Take time in the coming week to memorize this passage from John 8:31–32:

> To the Jews who had believed him, Jesus said, "If you hold to my teaching, you are really my disciples. Then you will know the truth, and the truth will set you free."

FIVE DEADLY LIES

REFLECTIONS FROM SESSION 1

1. If you have been battling against the temptation to have negative private conversations, how are you doing at replacing negative self-talk with the positive truth that comes from God?
2. If you took time to memorize and reflect on John 8:31–32, how has the truth of Jesus' words impacted the way you talk to yourself?

THE BIG PICTURE

Certain well-worn phrases set off my truth-detecting sensors the moment I hear them. When someone looks at me with concern in his or her eyes and begins, "What I am about to communicate is going to hurt me more than it's going to hurt you," I automatically say to myself, "I doubt it. I don't think what you are about to say will really hurt you more than it's going to hurt me. I think I'm being prepared for a confrontation that might hurt me a whole lot."

When I'm sitting in a plane on the runway and a voice over the intercom says, "Ladies and gentlemen, we're experiencing a mechanical problem in the cockpit, but we expect to be leaving the gate in just a few minutes," a sensor goes off in my mind. I find myself saying, "I seriously doubt that. I bet we won't be leaving for another half an hour."

We all have our list of phrases that trip our truth-detector button. When someone says, "No matter what happens tonight, I'll still respect you in the morning," the truth detector starts beeping. The dentist stands over you with an arsenal of weapons in his hands and says, "You won't feel a thing." Beep! "He's an honest politician." Beep! "I have my drinking under control. I don't have a problem." Beep! Beep! Beep! It seems the split second we hear certain phrases our truth detectors begin warning us of danger.

There is a spirit of error in this world. There is also a spirit of truth. We've all been burned by the spirit of error before, so we need to stay alert. When certain phrases trip our truth sensors, we need to raise our consciousness and prepare ourselves for action.

A WIDE ANGLE VIEW

1 What are some of the statements that trip your truth-detector switch?

A BIBLICAL PORTRAIT

Read Psalm 15:1–4

2 This passage paints a picture of a person who can enter God's presence freely. Describe what this person looks like.

3

In verse 2 we are called to speak the truth from the core of our heart. What does it mean to speak the truth within your own heart?

SHARPENING THE FOCUS

Read Snapshot "I Could Never Do That!"

I COULD NEVER DO THAT!

One deadly lie we tell ourselves is, "I could never do that." A new opportunity or challenge faces us at work, school, home, church, or someplace else and without even thinking we reflexively say, "Oh, I could never do that." A cigarette smoker really wants to quit but hopelessly says, "I could never do it." Someone struggling with eating patterns looks in the mirror and says, "I could never lose the weight I want to get rid of." Another person thinks about her desire to develop her abilities by going back to school or taking some private lessons but decides not to pursue this goal because she convinces herself, "I could never do it." Another person dreams of using his gifts or talents for ministry but does not even try because he has come to believe the deceptive secret lie he holds in his heart: "I could never do that."

What's even worse than saying the phrase "I could never do that," is believing it. We often buy this lie without processing it through truth filters. When we hear ourselves say, "I could never do that," we should hear bells, whistles, and sirens. Our truth detectors should beep so loud that we have to stop and ask where the lie is coming from.

4

We all have dreams and desires in our lives that get stomped down by the lie, "I could never do that." What is one area of your life in which you have battled this lie or are presently battling it?

What can your small group members do to help you fulfill your dream or desire in one area of your life?

Read Snapshot "That Would Be Terrible!"

THAT WOULD BE TERRIBLE!

Another deadly lie goes like this—"Oh, that would be just terrible." This lie paralyzes us by focusing on the exaggerated consequences of a minor slip up. Someone says, "If I went to the party in pants and all the other women were wearing dresses, that would be just terrible." Another person says, "If I play volleyball at the picnic and miss a few hits, that would be just terrible. I would be so embarrassed." Others think, "If I go to the swimming party and people see that I'm carrying an extra five pounds, that would just be terrible" or "If I stand up in a group to say something and it doesn't come out just right, that would be just terrible."

At the root of this lie is our intense pressure to please all of the people all of the time. We need to give this expectation up and liberate ourselves. We can't please all the people all the time, and God wants us to know that it is not wise to even try. When we are anxious about what might happen, what people might think, or how terrible the results will be, we are buying into a deadly lie.

---

5 What is an area of your life in which you are avoiding doing something because of the lie, "That would be just terrible"?

Tell about a time you overcame your fear of the lie, "That would be just terrible," and found out it was not so terrible after all.

Read Snapshot "I Need This!"

I NEED THIS!

Another deadly lie is "I need this" or "I need that." I remember a commercial I saw in the middle of a cold Chicago winter. It showed a man coming in from a bitter snowstorm. The ad was about a Florida vacation. The man cried out, "I *need* it bad!" Another commercial showed a woman with three remote control changers in her hand. She comes to the appliance store and says, "Can't somebody combine all these controls? I *need* to have one control instead of three." Advertisers and marketers have become very adept at convincing us that our wants are actually needs. We end up walking around saying, "I *need* a suit, a blouse, a VCR, a cellular phone, new golf clubs, a new car, a bigger house!" Our needs and wants can get easily confused.

6 What one thing are you seeking right now with an "I need it" mentality?

What will it take for you to be honest and move this item from your "need" to your "want" list?

Read Snapshot "God Will Never Forgive You for That!"

GOD WILL NEVER FORGIVE YOU FOR THAT!

One of the most deadly lies in the arsenal of the Evil One is when we say to ourselves, "God will never forgive me for that." Every person has been affected by this lie at one time or another. I remember meeting with a Christian leader who voluntarily confessed a series of personal sins to me. He was a knowledgeable and godly man who had taught the Bible and had a good knowledge of biblical truth. He'd been in Christian leadership for many years and had helped other wayward believers back onto the Christian path. But the day I met with him he looked tired and defeated. He said, "I feel like giving up." Then he said the words that we've all said to ourselves, "I feel so dirty. I feel so stained." In a dozen different ways, he said to me, "God will never forgive me for what I have done." He knew the truth, but he was believing a deadly lie.

When you believe this lie, a dark cloud hangs over your head. When you pray, all you can see is the depth of your sin. Your whole outlook on life changes. You can feel defeated, discouraged, even physically beaten down. I wonder how many of us buy into this lie? How many of us are tortured by it?

7 React to this statement made by a follower of Christ: "I have lied to my boss, neglected my children, and cheated on my spouse. There is no way God could ever forgive me. I am too dirty to experience God's love and cleansing."

Read Snapshot "God Couldn't Do Much Through Someone Like Me!"

GOD COULDN'T DO MUCH THROUGH SOMEONE LIKE ME!

 Some lies are so subtle we hardly know we're having a private conversation about them. One such lie is, "God probably could not do much through someone like me." When we see gifted and talented people around us we often shrink back and say to ourselves, "I am so average. I could never do the kinds of things that other people do." When we believe this lie we start saying, "I have nothing to contribute to the kingdom of God. There's no difference I could make. Let the talented people shine. Who needs my little flicker?"

This is a lie. Everyone who has admitted his or her sin and received Jesus Christ has been adopted into the family of God. God has plans for you to be productive and fruitful in His kingdom. There is no one else just like you in all the world. There is no one who has your personality, background, life experiences, or blend of gifts and skills. God has plans that can be carried out only by someone like you.

When you believe this, you will learn to present yourself to God and say, "God, please use me in some way. Touch a life through me. Show me how my life can matter more. Make a difference through me. I'm available. I'm reporting for duty."

8 What is one thing God is doing in your life today that you once believed was impossible?

PUTTING YOURSELF IN THE PICTURE

Fighting Lies with the Truth

There are five verses absolutely essential for all followers of Christ to commit to memory. Commit yourself to learning these verses in the coming weeks.

> "Come now, let us reason together," says the LORD. "Though your sins are like scarlet, they shall be as white as snow; though they are red as crimson, they shall be like wool."
>
> *Isaiah 1:18*

> . . . For I will forgive their wickedness and will remember their sins no more.
>
> *Jeremiah 31:34*

> . . . as far as the east is from the west, so far has he removed our transgressions from us.
>
> *Psalm 103:12*

> In him we have redemption through his blood, the forgiveness of sins, in accordance with the riches of God's grace . . .
>
> *Ephesians 1:7*

> If we confess our sins, he is faithful and just and will forgive us our sins and purify us from all unrighteousness.
>
> *1 John 1:9*

Maybe I Could Do That

Identify one thing you have been avoiding because you have been listening to the deadly lie, "I could never do that." If you have been held back because of a lie, pray for God to give you courage and strength to move forward in this area of your life. Set a specific goal to take steps toward starting something you have been afraid to try. Have at least one Christian friend pray for you and encourage you along the way.

TRUTH OR CONSEQUENCES

REFLECTIONS FROM SESSION 2

1. If you took time to memorize the passages listed in session two, would you recite one of the verses for your group and communicate what it means to you?
2. If you tried something new in an effort to battle the "I could never do that" lie, describe what it was like to take this step forward.

THE BIG PICTURE

One day when I was getting ready to step out of the shower at the YMCA where I work out, I noticed another man step out ahead of me. After making sure no one was watching, he grabbed *my* towel, dried himself, threw the towel on the floor, and then headed for the locker room. I couldn't believe it!

I was upset by his action, and being the forthright, fearless, outspoken, born activist I am, I said . . . absolutely nothing. On the inside, however, I was raging. "Excuse me, mister. That was my towel you just profaned. And I am more than a little perturbed about it!"

The man didn't know it was my towel he had just ripped off, so when I entered the locker room, he tried to engage me in friendly conversation—the stock market, the Bears players' strike, the weekend, the weather forecast. What did I do? I joined in the conversation, graciously submerging my feelings about what he had done. We dressed and parted ways.

But, do you know what? The next time I see that man, the first thought that's going to cross my mind is, *Why did he swipe my towel?* That man doesn't know it, but there's a major blockage in our relationship. Why didn't I just say, "Excuse me, sir, that's my towel"? or "Sir, did you forget your towel? I'll be happy to get you one." Why didn't I engage myself in the situation honestly? I'll tell you why. Because it's human nature to prefer peacekeeping over truth-telling. Most of us will do almost anything to avoid conflict.

A WIDE ANGLE VIEW

1   Describe in vivid detail a time you were burning to tell the truth but decided not to.

What were some of the results of that decision?

A BIBLICAL PORTRAIT

Read Ephesians 4:14–16, 25

2   How can speaking the truth, even when it is hard or painful, be an expression of love?

3

In this passage we are called to "put off falsehood and speak truthfully." What are some of the common falsehoods spoken in the following places:

- In the marketplace

- In the home

- In the church

- In the political arena

SHARPENING THE FOCUS

Read Snapshot "Peacekeeping vs. Truth-Telling"

PEACEKEEPING VS. TRUTH-TELLING

Honesty is essential for authentic relationships. This is true of friendships, marriages, work relationships, and every other kind of relationship. Too often we buy the lie that making peace is better than telling the truth. From our childhood we were taught to "shake hands and make up." Too often this process is an effort to solve a problem without ever addressing what it is. For too long we have tried to pretend everything is fine, when the truth is that there are still battle scars that need to be healed.

4 How do you respond when you are in situations where you want to tell the truth but you know that truth-telling will stir up problems, rock the "relational boat," and break the peace?

5 Tell about an instance when you risked telling a hard truth and found that, with time, it deepened the relationship.

Read Snapshot "Pseudocommunity"

PSEUDOCOMMUNITY

A relationship preserved through a consistent commitment to avoid telling the truth is counterfeit peace. It may have the appearance of peace, it may look like community, it may even feel like a real, authentic, communal relationship, but it is not. The relationship's appearance is deceiving and the community experienced in it is extremely shallow. In reality, it is a pseudocommunal relationship. In pseudocommunal relationships, feelings beg to be shared that never are. Misunderstandings arise that aren't dealt with. Doubts creep in about the integrity of the other person, but it seems safer to just let it go.

6 Describe what a pseudocommunal relationship looks like in *one* of these areas:

- Daily conversations
- Handling a difference of opinion
- Expressing appreciation

7 Identify one relationship you have right now that is in pseudocommunity because it lacks the transparency of truth-telling. What is keeping you from telling the truth in this relationship?

Read Snapshot "The Tunnel of Chaos"

THE TUNNEL OF CHAOS

Skiers know that if they want to drive from Denver to Vail, Colorado, they have to go through the Eisenhower Tunnel. It doesn't matter how much they dislike tunnels; if they want to make it to Vail, they have to go through that tunnel. Likewise, no matter how unpleasant the tunnel of chaos is, there's no other route to authentic relationships. One person in the relationship may decide to leave the counterfeit peace of pseudocommunity by revealing a long-concealed wound that hampers the relationship. Entering this tunnel is scary, but he cares about the relationship and wants to improve it. So he takes the risk.

In the tunnel of chaos hurts are unburied, hostilities are revealed, and tough questions are asked. What happens next? Sometimes the counterfeit peace shatters in an explosion of hostility that feels terrible. But when we get through this time of turmoil we find ourselves beyond pseudocommunity, entering into real community with the people in our lives.

8 Entering the tunnel of chaos is a choice each of us must make if we are to enter into communal relationships. But the truth is, many of us choose to stay in the safe harbor of pseudocommunal relationships. What are some possible risks of entering the tunnel of chaos in your relationships and what are the potential benefits?

Possible Risks   *Potential Benefits*

_____   _____

_____   _____

_____   _____

_____   _____

_____   _____

_____   _____

9 Who is one person in your life right now with whom you need to enter the tunnel of chaos if you are going to discover true community?

How can your small group members support and pray for you as you undertake this challenge?

PUTTING YOURSELF IN THE PICTURE

A COMMITMENT TO ENTER THE TUNNEL

Bring up on the screen of your imagination one key relationship in your life. It could be your spouse, someone you are dating, a family member, a friend, a coworker, or a fellow follower of Christ. Once you have a picture of that person in your mind, ask yourself this question, "Am I telling the truth to this person? Am I in pseudocommunity or real community? Is my primary goal to just keep the peace and not rock the boat? Is there a grievance or a hidden hurt that needs to be dealt with? Is there distrust?" Take time to be brutally honest with yourself and God about this relationship.

If you are in a pseudocommunal relationship with this person, you need to realize that if you stay in pseudocommunity long enough, the relationship is probably going to deteriorate and could eventually die. Make a decision to get together with this person very soon. Commit yourself to sit down with them and say, "I don't mean for this to be an upsetting conversation. I really don't. But I have to tell you some truthful things that might be difficult for me to say and hard for you to hear. It might cause some turmoil and chaos, but I am willing to take the risk for the sake of our relationship. I know that if we can negotiate the chaos and hang in and talk truthfully with each other, we can emerge from the other side of the tunnel in a truly communal relationship. It will be worth it. Let's trust God and see."

It would be wise to have at least one other believer praying for you and encouraging you to follow through on this commitment.

LEARNING FROM OTHERS

Take time in the coming week to contact another follower of Christ who you trust and respect. Be sure this person is committed to truth-telling and transparency in his or her own relationships. Ask this person to tell you about the scriptural truths and life experiences that have brought him or her to the place of being committed to truth-telling.

GAMES PEOPLE PLAY

REFLECTIONS FROM SESSION 3

1. If you took the courageous step of entering the tunnel of chaos with someone you have been in pseudocommunity with, tell your small group members what you have learned from this experience.
2. If you met with someone who is a truth-teller and asked that person what scriptural truths and life experiences moved him or her to this place, relay to your group what you learned from that person's wisdom.

THE BIG PICTURE

In our effort to build authentic relationships, sometimes we try to take shortcuts. Rather than go through the tunnel of chaos, we try other methods of communication. Rather than speaking the truth in a clear and loving manner, we use subtle tactics and sneak attacks. Ask yourself if you recognize any of these characters:

Henry the Hint-Dropper—He wants community but tries to build it with carefully placed hints and statements that make his point without ever really saying what is on his mind.

Mary the Manipulator—She knows what she wants in her relationships but can't seem to look people in the eye and state what is on her mind. Instead, she nags and pressures others in an effort to get them to conform to what she feels they should be doing.

Gary the Guilt-Tripper—He likes to use phrases like, "After all I have done for you" and "If you really cared about me, you would . . ." Rather than seek real community he settles for getting his way through coercion.

Ivan the Intimidator—He also wants community, but in his frustration and impatience resorts to pressure tactics, temper tantrums, and even occasional threats. He may get his way, but there is no real authenticity in this kind of a relationship.

Sara the Stonewaller—When her feelings get hurt, she pouts around until someone notices. She pushes out her lower lip, stomps around, and slams a few doors to communicate her displeasure. When someone finally responds to her subtle clues and asks, "Sara, are you okay?" she responds with a short, "I'm just fine!" and stomps off with her bottom lip dragging on the ground.

A WIDE ANGLE VIEW

1   What are some of the shortcuts you have seen people using to communicate what they are feeling *without* really telling the truth?

A BIBLICAL PORTRAIT

Read John 4:7–26

2   We are all familiar with the games people play to avoid telling the truth. Jesus never played games; as a matter of fact, He always spoke the truth. In this passage, how does Jesus tell the truth? Respond to *one* of the following areas of truth:

- How did Jesus speak the truth about Himself?
- How did Jesus speak the truth about the Samaritan woman's past?

- How did Jesus speak the truth about the Samaritan woman's spiritual condition and need?
- How did Jesus speak the truth about worship?
- How did Jesus speak the truth about the spiritual needs of all people?

3 How does the example of Jesus' truth-telling stand in stark contrast to the games people still play today?

SHARPENING THE FOCUS

Read Snapshot "Henry the Hint-Dropper"

HENRY THE HINT-DROPPER

Meet Henry the Hint-Dropper. He has been in a pseudocommunal relationship with his wife ever since she decided to reenter the marketplace after the kids began school. For six months she has been working hard in the marketplace. She's having some difficulty juggling work, two kids, a husband, a house, meals, and all the other elements of her life. Henry is having a hard time adjusting to her new schedule and he's feeling a little overlooked and neglected by his once-attentive wife.

Henry submerges his hurt feelings, refusing to be transparent and tell the truth about how he's feeling. Instead, he stays in pseudocommunity by playing the hint-dropping game. Finally detachment and bitterness set in. He wants to get back into intimacy with his wife, but he is not willing to start telling the truth. He's not going to sit down and say, "Honey, I'm hurt. I feel neglected. I know you're juggling a lot, but we can't go on like this. What solution can we come up with together?"

Instead, one night while his wife is scrambling around the kitchen trying to get dinner on the table, Henry looks over the top of his newspaper and casually says, "Honey, you know, I'm thinking about buying some stock in Stouffer's frozen dinners." His wife says, "What do you mean by that, Henry?" And he says, "Oh, nothing. I just heard that there are some takeover rumors." Later on in the evening, he tells his wife that a friend at work gets romantic notes tucked in his pockets three times a week. He says, "That's some woman Frank married." A little later Henry says, "I saw an ad about a new business in town called 'Rent a Wife.' I thought I might look into it!" Henry's motto has become "Subtlety is the best policy."

4 How do you see Henry the Hint-Dropper in yourself as you relate to others?

How do you see hint-dropping tactics as others relate to you?

5 What are some of the results you have seen in your relationships when hint-dropping replaces truth-telling?

Read Snapshot "Mary the Manipulator"

MARY THE MANIPULATOR

Mary the Manipulator would love to move out of pseudocommunity toward a true communal relationship, but she is not willing to face a real truth-telling session. She doesn't want to have a real heart-to-heart with her husband and risk rocking the boat. Mary doesn't think the problem in her marriage is about communication; the problem is her husband. You see, Mary got hitched to a mild-mannered, peace-loving, laid-back man who is just not as motivated or as energetic as Mary thinks he should be.

In Mary's mind, the standard energy measurement by which all humans should be evaluated is directly related to her own personal energy level. She knows just how motivated and energetic everybody ought to be. So, after a few years of being married to a man who only uses fifty-watt lightbulbs, she is experiencing some built-up frustrations and pent-up anger. But rather than attempting a truth-telling session, she's got a better idea. She is going to "should" him.

She says, "Carl, you should get up and do something. Every time I see you, you are just vegetating" or "You should spend more time with Jimmy. He's having trouble with his math again" or "You shouldn't spend so much time watching TV" or "You should take up jogging." She's like a recording. "Carl, you should. Carl, you ought. Carl, you shouldn't."

6 How do you see the tactics of Mary the Manipulator in your relationships?

7 What is the result in a relationship when a person resorts to manipulation instead of truth-telling?

Read Snapshot "Gary the Guilt-Tripper"

GARY THE GUILT-TRIPPER

Meet Gary the Guilt-Tripper. He refuses to enter the tunnel of chaos and tell the truth. Instead, he keeps on playing games. "Gee Fred, after all I've done for you, I ask this one thing. Won't you do it for me?" Or "Oh Jim, after all I've given up for you. What do you mean you can't go with me? I was planning on you going. Well, I'll probably go all by myself. If I get mugged or killed when I'm by myself, hey, no problem. My premiums are paid. If I never see you again, it's been nice." Or how about this one? "Well, if that's all your mother and I mean to you, okay then. You'll hear no complaints from us." When Gary makes a request of his pastor that he can't fulfill, he says, "No problem, Reverend. I'll just find a church where the pastor has time for his people."

8 How have you experienced the "guilt-trip" approach to communication in *one* of these areas:

- In the workplace
- In your home growing up
- In a friendship
- In the church

9 What were the consequences of this approach to communication?

PUTTING YOURSELF IN THE PICTURE

A Process for Developing Transparency

Identify one specific relationship in which you are avoiding the tunnel of chaos. No matter what shortcut you are trying to take, commit yourself to walking through this process in an effort to open the door for transparency in relationship and real community.

First, *identify the real obstacle*. Before you blurt out an unedited, "Hey, buddy, I've got a problem with you," take time to determine the real issue. Is it hurt feelings? A history of dishonesty? Do you feel neglected or misunderstood? Identify it, then talk to the Lord about it. Sort it out. Some people find it helpful to organize their thoughts on paper.

Second, *arrange to meet the person face-to-face as soon as possible*. Jesus tells us that if we have a problem in a relationship we should meet with that person in private (Matt. 18:15). A phone call is not enough—without visual cues, conversation can lead to greater misunderstanding. Paul says we should do this as soon as possible. "Do not let the sun go down while you are still angry" (Eph. 4:26). The longer we stay in pseudocommunity, the more the relationship deteriorates.

Third, when you meet, *affirm the relationship before you open up the agenda*. If you're meeting with your spouse, say, "Look, honey, I love you and I value our relationship. I want our marriage to be all it can be, and I believe it has the potential to be mutually satisfying in every way. But I need to talk to you about a few things that are standing in the way."

Fourth, *make observations rather than accusations*. Human beings tend to do what animals do when they're attacked. They strike back. Don't put up your dukes and start throwing punches. Say, "Look, I'm feeling hurt by some things you did. You probably didn't intend to hurt me, but that's what I feel. Can we talk about it?" Or "I'm sensing a change in our relationship. I don't feel as comfortable with you anymore. I'd like your input." This approach opens the way for dialogue that can lead to true community.

HONEST TO GOD, OURSELVES, AND OTHERS

Identify which of these games you are most likely to play:

- The "hint-dropping" game
- The "manipulation" game
- The "guilt-trip" game

As you honestly identify negative and unhealthy patterns in your communication with others, admit this to God. Tell Him that you are sorry you are playing games instead of telling the truth. Next, acknowledge these unhealthy patterns to your-self. Allow yourself to identify the relationships and situations that most often lead to game playing in your communication. Finally, go to the person you have been playing games with and tell them you are sorry. Be honest. Say, "I have been heaping guilt on you and I am sorry. You mean too much to me for game playing. I want you to know that in the future I am committed to telling the truth with no games."

EXPRESSING POSITIVE EMOTIONS

REFLECTIONS FROM SESSION 4

1. If you committed yourself to walking through a process of developing transparency in a specific relationship through telling the truth instead of playing games, tell your group how you are doing at keeping this commitment and how your actions have impacted this relationship.
2. If you have taken time to identify an area in your communication where you have been playing a game instead of telling the truth, tell your group members what you have learned about yourself and how they can pray for you as you seek to be a truth-teller.

THE BIG PICTURE

Some time ago I had lunch with a friend. Throughout the meal this man spoke very highly of his son, who had started a new business venture. He told me how sharp his boy was and how great he felt about his abilities and capabilities. It was a treat to hear a dad speak with such admiration and affirmation about his son.

A month or so later, I happened to spend a few hours with the man's son. As we had lunch together, this young man spent the better part of the lunch pouring out his heart to me. He said he was utterly discouraged and almost defeated because he sensed no affirmation from his father. In his own words, he found it almost impossible to win even one word of praise from his dad. He related to me how defeated he was about not knowing how his dad really felt about him.

Finally, when he stopped, I said, "I don't want to talk out of place, but this is a shock to me." I told him, "I was with your dad less than a month ago and all he did was sing your praises to me. He told me how he loved you and how proud of you he was. He told me how much he respected you and what a great job you were doing in your business." I assured him of his father's love and affirmation.

This young man slammed his fist down on the restaurant table and said, "Why would he tell you and not tell me?" I could clearly see the pain this young man was feeling.

A WIDE ANGLE VIEW

1 Why do you think this father would freely tell others about his love and respect for his son but not tell the son himself?

Why do you think the son was hurt and angry when he heard his father's praise from another person?

A BIBLICAL PORTRAIT

Read Luke 17:11–19

2 What impresses you about the Samaritan leper in this story?

How can his actions and words function as an example in your relationship with Jesus?

3 Ten lepers were healed, but only one came back to express gratitude and appreciation. What do you think stood in the way of the other nine coming back to respond to Jesus?

What stands in the way of your expressing appreciation and positive emotions?

SHARPENING THE FOCUS

Read Snapshot "A Look"

A LOOK

Again and again the Bible calls us to build each other up by expressing positive emotions. In a hard-hearted world, we are called to express love to each other. In this session we will be looking at three practical ways we can express positive emotions.

It is often said that "the eyes are the window of the soul." We are all familiar with expressions like, "If looks could kill," or "I gave them the evil eye." We can decimate somebody by the way we look at them, or we can build somebody up with a look, a smile, a wink, or a nod.

Have you ever watched little kids playing on a sports team? From time to time, one of the kids who has been involved in an important play will run near the sideline looking over at the parents, family members, friends, and coaches. What are their little eyes searching for as they scan the sidelines? Quite simply, a look of encouragement. A look of praise. A look of affirmation. They know that a glance can convey an enormous amount of affirmation. The truth is, no matter how old we are, we are still saying, "Daddy, watch me!" as we seek out those people who will acknowledge us with a look of love and affirmation.

4 Describe a picture you hold in your heart of a time someone gave you a look of love. Why does this picture mean so much to you?

5 What is it in a person's look that builds you up and affirms you?

What is it in a person's look that can tear you down or bring pain to your heart?

Read Snapshot "A Word"

A WORD

Mark Twain said, "I can live two months on one good compliment." Sometimes a simple phrase will seal itself in our memories for a lifetime. Certain expressions of encouragement act as an emergency power supply when our emotional batteries run low.

No one has to remind us how powerful the spoken word can be. Words can be destructive or constructive. James 3:10 says, "Out of the same mouth come praise and cursing." Most of us can recall, word for word, a time when somebody turned on us and spoke in a way that cut all the way to our heart. By the same token, most of us could recite, word for word, a time when someone spoke words of commendation, approval, affirmation, or encouragement.

We all know how much what we say matters. When we hear words of affirmation and love, we lock them into the memory log of our minds and play them over and over again.

6 We all have an "audio log" in our memories of the encouraging and affirming things people have said to us. Relate one of those memories and communicate why it means so much to you.

7 Who is one person in your life who needs to hear a word of encouragement and love from you?

In what ways can your group members pray for you as you commit to honestly expressing your emotions to this person in the coming days?

Read Snapshot "A Touch"

A TOUCH

If you've studied the life of Jesus at all, you know that Jesus often did more than offer looks of love and words of encouragement. He also had a habit of touching people. The Gospels record that Jesus touched children, blind people, lepers, outcasts, and many others. Jesus was drawn to reach out and physically touch those He was with. Even though He could have just spoken a word and brought healing, He often touched those who were broken, sick, and in spiritual turmoil.

Near the end of His life, Jesus applied His touch to His disciples by actually washing their dirty feet. Jesus knew that Judas, one of the disciples sitting at the table that night, would soon betray Him, yet despite this knowledge, He realized the incredible mark that could be made by a loving touch. And He calls us to follow His example.

8 Describe a time when someone reached out to you with a touch of love. What was it about their actions that made you feel loved?

9 Who is one person in your life who currently needs a touch of love?

What would be an appropriate expression of love toward this person?

PUTTING YOURSELF IN THE PICTURE

A WORD OF AFFIRMATION

Let me offer five quick summary statements about spoken words of affirmation.

1. *If you feel it, say it.* Even if you are not articulate, say it anyway.
2. *Do not wait for the ideal time, because it never comes.* You may have to make sneak attacks sometimes where you just grab someone and say, "You are doing a great job" or " I love you" or "You are important to me." If you are waiting for the time to be right, that time will never come.

3. *Be very specific in your encouragement.* The more specific you can be, the more meaningful the encouragement is.
4. *Do not exaggerate with false praise or empty flattery.* The Bible says, "A flattering mouth works ruin" (Prov. 26:28).
5. *If you cannot say it because you just are not a verbal person, write it.* If you are uncomfortable putting your feelings into spoken words, write them down and slip somebody a note. However you choose to do it, the key is to be sure to express what you feel.

A Challenge for the Courageous

In this lesson we have reflected on the importance of expressing positive emotions. Here is a challenge for the courageous of heart. Set a goal to express positive emotion on all three levels. Seek to be very specific.

Showing Positive Emotions with a Look:

The person I will show positive emotions to: _____

How I will express myself: _____

_____

When I will do this: _____

Who will pray for me and encourage me to follow through:

_____

Showing Positive Emotions with a Word:

The person I will show positive emotions to: _____

How I will express myself: _____

_____

When I will do this: _____

Who will pray for me and encourage me to follow through:

_____

Showing Positive Emotions with a Touch:

The person I will show positive emotions to: _____

How I will express myself: _____

_____

When I will do this: _____

Who will pray for me and encourage me to follow through:

_____

HEARING THE TRUTH

REFLECTIONS FROM SESSION 5

1. If you used the tools you learned in the last session to begin speaking encouraging words to others, tell your group members how you are developing your ability to speak words of affirmation. How have others received your encouraging words?
2. If you made a point of expressing positive emotions to someone in your life through a look, a word, or a touch, how did this experience make you feel? How do you think it made them feel?

THE BIG PICTURE

Some years ago we built a much needed chapel on our church campus. As is our custom whenever we begin a new building on our campus, we had a company analyze the soil to determine the quality of the ground where we planned to build. After those soil borings were completed and analyzed, one of our construction guys said, "Well, do you want to hear the truth about the soil under the chapel or should I lie and make you feel good?" It was tempting for us to want to believe that all was well under that well-manicured lawn, but we were committed to building a structure that would stand for a long time, so we said, "You better tell us the truth."

"The soil is bad," the man replied. "Tons of it are going to have to be removed, and then new dirt is going to have to be brought in and compacted. If we do it right, the chapel will stand firmly for a long time." Those words were both disappointing and expensive. But when we look at that chapel standing there all these years later, we're glad we requested, received, and responded to the truth about that soil.

Some years ago my mother saw her doctor for a routine physical. In her typical, easygoing fashion she asked, "So how am I doing, Doc?" The doctor responded with words something like, "Mrs. Hybels, do you want the truth, or do you want me to lie and make you feel good?" Not many of us would be foolish enough to close our ears to the truth if our health and future were really at stake, so my mother said, "Tell me the truth." The doctor told her she had cancer and that she had to have major surgery as soon as possible. The family gathered around her and she had the surgery. When it was over she was given a virtually clean bill of health. She was very glad that she requested, received, and responded to the truth of her condition.

Whether you're building marriages, families, friendships, business relationships, or any other relationship, it pays to hear the truth. It's worth it even if the hard words upset apple carts, rock boats, and cut you to the core! Relationships built on anything less than truth are destined for disaster.

A WIDE ANGLE VIEW

1   Tell about a time you heard the truth, responded to it, and were glad you did.

Tell about a time you refused to hear the truth or did not respond to the truth you heard, and regretted this decision.

A BIBLICAL PORTRAIT

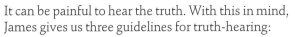

Read James 1:19–20

2

It can be painful to hear the truth. With this in mind,
James gives us three guidelines for truth-hearing:

- Be quick to listen
- Be slow to speak
- Be slow to become angry

*How do these three guidelines function together to help us in
the process of hearing the truth?*

SHARPENING THE FOCUS

Read Snapshot "Hearing the Truth, Even When It Hurts"

HEARING THE TRUTH, EVEN WHEN IT HURTS

When someone hits a major-league line drive of truth at our hearts, it is easy to respond reflexively. The problem is that our instinctive response is rarely healthy. I find there are three primary knee-jerk responses when a person tries to speak a hard truth.

1. *Denial.* Our denial weapons are activated while the other person is only beginning to get to the point. When someone says, "I'd like to talk to you about something," and we detect that hard words might be coming, we begin thinking, "Whatever issue this person is about to bring to my attention, he's got the wrong person. I don't know what it is yet, but I would never do whatever he thinks I did."

2. *Retaliation.* After we begin to deny any fault, the retaliation machine gets fired up. We say to ourselves, "If this person hits too close to home, I'm going to point out to him that he hasn't lived a perfect life either. If we're going to start dragging out the laundry, I've got some access to his dirty clothes basket. I am more than willing to sink to whatever level is needed to neutralize this attack."

3. *Rationalization.* Finally, our rationalization kicks in. We think, "There are 250 ex-murderers loose on the street and you're coming after me for some misdemeanor?" We tell ourselves that whatever we did, we certainly had good reason and it is unfair for anyone to bring up such minor faults in us. When the hard truth comes flying toward us, we can easily put up defenses that will keep us from having to deal with the truth.

3 Every once in awhile during a baseball game a batter will hit a line drive right back at the pitcher at over one hundred mph. In that fraction of a second, the pitcher will throw up his glove, responding reflexively in an effort to protect himself. When someone speaks a hard truth to you, what are some of your reflexive responses?

4 How do you see patterns of *one* of these responses (denial, retaliation, rationalization, or any others) in your relationships when it comes time to hear the hard truth?

5 If these responses stand in the way of hearing the truth, what is the antidote to each?

Response	*Antidote*
Denial	_____
Retaliation	_____
Rationalization	_____

Read Snapshot "Hearing the Truth, Even When It Feels Good!"

HEARING THE TRUTH, EVEN WHEN IT FEELS GOOD!

Not only do we need to hear the truth when it hurts, but we also need to receive and respond to positive words from others. You would think this would be easy, but often it is not. We all have had experiences when we have encouraged or complimented someone only to have them refuse our words or brush them off. You know the routine:

"Jamie, you played so well at your piano recital."

"Oh no, I didn't. I was awful. I played like I was wearing mittens. I was so embarrassed."

It's frustrating, isn't it? It would seem like people should be open to positive and affirming words, but many often resist.

---

6 How do you usually respond when someone says something positive and affirming to you?

7 How do you want people to respond when you give them a truthful word of affirmation and encouragement?

Why is it hard to respond this way yourself?

8 What is a positive and affirming thing you want to tell a member of your small group right now?

Read Snapshot "Hearing the Truth from God"

HEARING THE TRUTH FROM GOD

There are many people who attend church regularly, and even take part in gatherings like small groups, who enjoy being around church without really being changed by God. They don't mind a little religion and occasional church services, but they don't want to meet Jesus face-to-face and have to deal with their own condition before a holy God. If this is the case in your life, you need to hear the truth from God's Word, the Bible.

The Bible says that you matter to God, and that He loves you more than words could describe. It also says that you're a moral failure in God's sight. You have sinned. You've said, thought, and done wrong things. This puts you at odds with God. No matter what you try to do to make up for the wrongs you have done, it's never going to be enough. The good news is that you can turn to Jesus Christ, who died on a sin-stained cross for you to pay for your sins. In Christ, you can find what you're looking for. Your search is not really for a church; what you need is a personal Savior.

God's Word says that if you spend your whole life putting off this decision and come to the point of your death, you will stand before a holy God without a Savior. If this happens, you will have to pay for the sins you've committed in hell for eternity. I know these are hard words, but they must be heard. You can deny what you know is true, you can crank up your rationalizer, and you can load up your retaliation machine, but it won't change the simple truth. You need Jesus as your Savior.

---

9 If you have come to the place where you have faced the hard truth of your own sinfulness and your need of Jesus as your Savior, what helped you come to this realization and face the truth?

How has facing this truth changed your life?

10

If you have not yet faced the truth about your need of Jesus as your Savior, what do you feel is standing in the way? (If you need to, pause and pair up with a partner and pray that God will open your heart to His truth.)

PUTTING YOURSELF IN THE PICTURE

AN EXTRA-CREDIT PROJECT

I want to give an extra-credit assignment to the stout of heart. This is just for the extravagant risk-takers. I challenge you to go to your spouse, parents, children, close friends, fellow worker, or some other trusted person and say, "Friend, what would you like to say to me if you knew that I wouldn't get defensive and angry with you for telling me the truth?" Pray in advance, prepare your heart, and commit yourself *not* to respond with denial, retaliation, or rationalization. Give the person a chance to speak the truth to you.

SPEAKING THE TRUTH

Commit yourself to speak at least one positive, uplifting, and encouraging truth to another person every day for the coming week. Don't let others brush off your affirming words. Be sure you follow through at least once a day with speaking a loving truth to a person in your life.

Leader's Notes

Leading a Bible discussion—especially for the first time—can make you feel both nervous and excited. If you are nervous, realize that you are in good company. Many biblical leaders, such as Moses, Joshua, and the apostle Paul, felt nervous and inadequate to lead others (see, for example, 1 Cor. 2:3). Yet God's grace was sufficient for them, just as it will be for you.

Some excitement is also natural. Your leadership is a gift to the others in the group. Keep in mind, however, that other group members also share responsibility for the group. Your role is simply to stimulate discussion by asking questions and encouraging people to respond. The suggestions listed below can help you to be an effective leader.

Preparing to Lead

1. Ask God to help you understand and apply the passage to your own life. Unless that happens, you will not be prepared to lead others.
2. Carefully work through each question in the study guide. Meditate and reflect on the passage as you formulate your answers.
3. Familiarize yourself with the Leader's Notes for each session. These will help you understand the purpose of the session and will provide valuable information about the questions in the session. The Leader's Notes are not intended to be read to the group. These notes are primarily for your use as a group leader and for your preparation. However, when you find a section that relates well to your group, you may want to read a brief portion or encourage them to read this section at another time.
4. Pray for the various members of the group. Ask God to use these sessions to make you better disciples of Jesus Christ.
5. Before the first session, make sure each person has a study guide. Encourage them to prepare beforehand for each session.

LEADING THE SESSION

1. Begin the session on time. If people realize that the session begins on schedule, they will work harder to arrive on time.
2. At the beginning of your first time together, explain that these sessions are designed to be discussions, not lectures. Encourage everyone to participate, but realize some may be hesitant to speak during the first few sessions.
3. Don't be afraid of silence. People in the group may need time to think before responding.
4. Avoid answering your own questions. If necessary, rephrase a question until it is clearly understood. Even an eager group will quickly become passive and silent if they think the leader will do most of the talking.
5. Encourage more than one answer to each question. Ask, "What do the rest of you think?" or "Anyone else?" until several people have had a chance to respond.
6. Try to be affirming whenever possible. Let people know you appreciate their insights into the passage.
7. Never reject an answer. If it is clearly wrong, ask, "Which verse led you to that conclusion?" Or let the group handle the problem by asking them what they think about the question.
8. Avoid going off on tangents. If people wander off course, gently bring them back to the passage being considered.
9. Conclude your time together with conversational prayer. Ask God to help you apply those things that you learned in the session.
10. End on time. This will be easier if you control the pace of the discussion by not spending too much time on some questions or too little on others.

We encourage all small group leaders to use *Leading Life-Changing Small Groups* (Zondervan) by Bill Donahue and the Willow Creek Small Group Team while leading their group. Developed and used by Willow Creek Community Church, this guide is an excellent resource for training and equipping followers of Christ to effectively lead small groups. It includes valuable information on how to utilize fun and creative relationship-building exercises for your group; how to plan your meeting; how to share the leadership load by identifying, developing, and working with an "apprentice leader"; and how to find creative ways to do group prayer. In addition, the book includes material and tips on handling potential conflicts and difficult personalities, forming group covenants, inviting new members, improving listening skills, studying the Bible, and much more. Using *Leading Life-Changing Small Groups* will help you create a group that members love to be a part of.

Now let's discuss the different elements of this small group study guide and how to use them for the session portion of your group meeting.

THE BIG PICTURE

Each session will begin with a short story or overview of the lesson theme. This is called "The Big Picture" because it introduces the central theme of the session. You will need to read this section as a group or have group members read it on their own before discussion begins. Here are three ways you can approach this section of the small group session:

- As the group leader, read this section out loud for the whole group and then move into the questions in the next section, "A Wide Angle View." (You might read the first week, but then use the other two options below to encourage group involvement.)
- Ask a group member to volunteer to read this section for the group. This allows another group member to participate. It is best to ask someone in advance to give them time to read over the section before reading it to the group. It is also good to ask someone to volunteer, and not to assign this task. Some people do not feel comfortable reading in front of a group. After a group member has read this section out loud, move into the discussion questions.
- Allow time at the beginning of the session for each person to read this section silently. If you do this, be sure to allow enough time for everyone to finish reading so they can think about what they've read and be ready for meaningful discussion.

A WIDE ANGLE VIEW

This section includes one or more questions that move the group into a general discussion of the session topic. These questions are designed to help group members begin discussing the topic in an open and honest manner. Once the topic of the lesson has been established, move on to the Bible passage for the session.

A BIBLICAL PORTRAIT

This portion of the session includes a Scripture reading and one or more questions that help group members see how the theme of the session is rooted and based in biblical teaching. The Scripture reading can be handled just like "The Big Picture" section: You can read it for the group, have a group member read it, or allow time for silent reading. Make sure everyone has a Bible or that you have Bibles available for those who need them. Once you have read the passage, ask the question(s) in this section so that group members can dig into the truth of the Bible.

SHARPENING THE FOCUS

The majority of the discussion questions for the session are in this section. These questions are practical and help group members apply biblical teaching to their daily lives.

SNAPSHOTS

The "Snapshots" in each session help prepare group members for discussion. These anecdotes give additional insight to the topic being discussed. Each "Snapshot" should be read at a designated point in the session. This is clearly marked in the session as well as in the Leader's Notes. Again, follow the same format as you do with "The Big Picture" section and the "Biblical Portrait" section: Either you read the anecdote, have a group member volunteer to read, or provide time for silent reading. However you approach this section, you will find these anecdotes very helpful in triggering lively dialogue and moving discussion in a meaningful direction.

PUTTING YOURSELF IN THE PICTURE

Here's where you roll up your sleeves and put the truth into action. This portion is very practical and action-oriented. At the end of each session there will be suggestions for one or two ways group members can put what they've just learned into practice. Review the action goals at the end of each session and challenge group members to work on one or more of them in the coming week.

You will find follow-up questions for the "Putting Yourself in the Picture" section at the beginning of the next week's session. Starting with the second week, there will be time set aside at the beginning of the session to look back and talk about how you have tried to apply God's Word in your life since your last time together.

PRAYER

You will want to open and close your small group with a time of prayer. Occasionally, there will be specific direction within a session for how you can do this. Most of the time, however, you will need to decide the best place to stop and pray. You may want to pray or have a group member volunteer to begin the lesson with a prayer. Or you might want to read "The Big Picture" and discuss the "Wide Angle View" questions before opening in prayer. In some cases, it might be best to open in prayer after you have read the Bible passage. You need to decide where you feel an opening prayer best fits for your group.

When opening in prayer, think in terms of the session theme and pray for group members (including yourself) to be responsive to the truth of Scripture and the working of the Holy Spirit. If you have seekers in your group (people investigating Christianity but not yet believers) be sensitive to your expectations for group prayer. Seekers may not yet be ready to take part in group prayer.

Be sure to close your group with a time of prayer as well. One option is for you to pray for the entire group. Or you might allow time for group members to offer audible prayers that others can agree with in their hearts. Another approach would be to allow a time of silence for one-on-one prayers with God and then to close this time with a simple "Amen."

SECRET
CONVERSATIONS

JOHN 8:31–32, 42–47

INTRODUCTION

We all engage in self-talk—ongoing internal dialogues so natural that we barely notice them. Admittedly, many of these conversations are innocuous banterings that have minimal effect on the flow of our lives. But from time to time, we say things to ourselves that have a profound influence on what we believe and how we act. What we say is extremely important when it concerns highly sensitive matters of the heart. Those private conversations can change the entire direction of our lives.

THE BIG PICTURE

Take time to read this introduction with the group. There are suggestions for how this can be done in the beginning of the leader's section.

A WIDE ANGLE VIEW

A BIBLICAL PORTRAIT

Read John 8:31–32, 42–47

Questions Two & Three The Bible is very clear about who is prompting us to tell ourselves internal lies. In fact, Jesus Himself cleared up all the confusion on this issue by calling Satan not only a "liar" but the "Father of lies" (John 8:44). Satan's goal is to sabotage the work of God in the world and to undermine what God is doing in the lives of people. The Evil One starts his work in the heart because, as Proverbs 4:23 says, "Guard your heart, for it is the wellspring of life."

We need to increase our awareness of what we're saying to ourselves all day long in the areas of self-worth, personal competency, and spiritual matters. Whenever we sense we are having an internal dialogue about these critical matters, we need to ask ourselves about the origin of these thoughts and conversations. When they are lies, we know they come from the Enemy and we must resist them. On the other hand, truthful thoughts are from God and we must respond to them.

SHARPENING THE FOCUS

Read Snapshot "Secret Conversations About Your Self-Worth" before Question 4

Questions Four & Five The Bible is the final word on the subject of our personal worth. No matter what value your parents, relatives, teachers, friends, or even you put on yourself, the ultimate reality is the value God places on you! The Bible is full of truth about how much you matter to God. In Psalm 56 we read, in effect, "Oh Lord, You take notice of my walk and You take notice of my wanderings and You carefully keep record of each of my tears." This is God's way of saying there is immeasurable value placed on each one of us. There's not a road you travel or a tear you cry that He does not take note of.

Isaiah 43:1–2 says, "But now, this is what the LORD says—he who created you, O Jacob, he who formed you, O Israel: 'Fear not, for I have redeemed you; I have summoned you by name; you are mine. When you pass through the waters, I will be with you; and when you pass through the rivers, they will not sweep over you. When you walk through the fire, you will not be burned; the flames will not set you ablaze.'" Psalm 8:4–6 says, "what is man that you are mindful of him, the son of man that you care for him? You made him a little lower than the heavenly beings and crowned him with glory and honor. You made him ruler over the works of your hands; you put everything under his feet." God says that we are the crown of His creation and we matter more to Him than we could ever dream.

God treasures your uniqueness. He dreams of enabling you to become more than you could ever be without Him. You matter to Him. You need to learn to hear the truth about your self-worth. There is no room for running yourself into the ground. It's time that you start catching yourself in midsentence and start saying, "Wait a minute. I'm lying right now. What I'm saying about me is a lie. I've got to renounce this lie and replace it with the truth. I matter to God, and He sent his Son to die for me."

Read Snapshot "Secret Conversations About Personal Competency" before Question 6

Questions Six & Seven What have you been telling yourself lately about your competency? Has the I-can't-do-anything-right speech been floating around in your head? Have you had the nothing-I-do-works-out conversation with yourself? Have you recited the I-was-absent-on-the-day-God-distributed-talents speech? Isn't it time that you catch yourself and say, "Wait a minute, that's a lie"?

The Bible reminds us that we are fearfully and wonderfully made (Ps. 139:14). God has put within each of us some won-derful abilities to do certain kinds of things. Usually, with proper training and perseverance, we can increase our competency in those areas. We need to assess the abilities, talents, and gifts God has given us and say, "I don't need to compare myself to other people. Instead, I should just develop my own skills and abilities to their fullest potential. Thank You for making me a competent person in the areas I am gifted." This kind of self-talk is freeing.

Read Snapshot "Secret Conversations About Spiritual Matters" before Question 8

Questions Eight & Nine Every member of your small group needs to ask the million-dollar question, "Am I telling myself the truth about where I am spiritually?" I remember a man who looked me straight in the eye and said, "There's no Judgment Day. There's no heaven and there's no hell." And I said to him, "Friend, you're lying to yourself. You have a vested interest in lying to yourself because you know that you're not ready to face the Judgment Day. Deep down you know there is a heav-en and a hell and you are ill-prepared. You're facing an agoniz-ing decision of whether or not to speak the truth to yourself about these matters." My heart ached when I left that conver-sation. I thought about the thousands of people who go to church every Sunday but continue lying to themselves. They don't mean to. They're not even aware they're doing it. But they are lying to themselves about where they are spiritually.

When we meet God face-to-face the truth will come out. There will be no lies. No distortions. No deceit. In that day some will say, "I didn't lie to myself about spiritual matters. I knew of my sin and my need for a Savior. I knew of Jesus Christ, who offered to pay for my sins by what He did on the cross. And I repented. I entrusted my destiny and my sins to Jesus Christ." And God will say, "You told the truth to yourself and you did the truthful thing. Welcome home." The truth will be known.

But for others, when the truth comes out they will realize how wrong they were. They will have to say, "Deep down I knew the truth, but I lied to myself because I couldn't stand the pain of being ill-prepared before a holy God. I couldn't stand to deal with the discomfort of feeling condemned and needing forgiveness." The high price of those lies they told themselves during this life will cost them an eternity in hell.

Don't lie to yourself about your worth or your competency. And most of all, don't lie to yourself about spiritual matters. Speak the truth in your heart. It will make a difference in this life and for eternity.

PUTTING YOURSELF IN THE PICTURE

Tell group members you will be providing time at the beginning of the next meeting for them to discuss how they have put their faith into practice. Let them tell their stories. However, don't limit their interaction to the two options provided. They may have put themselves into the picture in some other way as a result of your study. Allow for honest and open communication.

Also, be clear that there will not be any kind of a "test" or forced reporting. All you are going to do is allow time for people to volunteer to talk about how they have applied what they learned in your last study. Some group members will feel pressured if they think you are going to make everyone provide a "report." You don't want anyone to skip the next group because they are afraid of having to say they did not follow up on what they learned from the prior session. Focus instead on providing a place for honest communication without creating pressure or fear of being embarrassed.

Every session from this point on will open with a look back at the "Putting Yourself in the Picture" section of the previous session.

FIVE DEADLY LIES
PSALM 15:1—4

INTRODUCTION

Most of us have learned that believing lies can lead to a lot of pain, heartache, and disappointment. In this session I want to identify five deadly lies we sometimes tell ourselves. These five lies wreak havoc in the minds of many, many people. They ought to immediately trip our truth detectors and set off bells, whistles, and sirens in our minds. We need to identify them, expose them, and discuss them so that whenever we hear them or say them to ourselves in private conversations, we will immediately respond, "That's one of those phrases I ought to watch out for."

THE BIG PICTURE

Take time to read this introduction with the group. There are suggestions for how this can be done in the beginning of the leader's section.

A BIBLICAL PORTRAIT

Read Psalm 15:1–4

SHARPENING THE FOCUS

Read Snapshot "I Could Never Do That!" before Question 4

Question Four Whenever you say, "Oh, I could never do that," stop. Ask yourself if you are speaking the truth. Are you absolutely sure you could never do it? Wouldn't it be more truthful to say, "Wait. Before I sentence myself to failure, I should remind myself of some basic truths about who God has made me to be."

Here are some basic truths about you that come straight from God's Word. Psalm 139:14 says, "I praise you because I am fearfully and wonderfully made; your works are wonderful, I know that full well." God has gifted you with unique skills and talents. You can develop those talents and accomplish things that will surprise and amaze you. Instead of being paralyzed by the fear of failure, simply take small steps in the direction God is leading. He'll help you along the way. The Bible also says, "I can do everything through Christ who gives me strength" (Phil. 4:13), and straight from the lips of Jesus, "What is impossible with men is possible with God" (Luke 18:27).

Let's make it a practice to speak truth in our hearts and fight against the deadly "I could never do that" lie. When we do, we will expand our talents, our minds, and our relationships. Most important, we can accomplish much more spiritually than we are at this time in our lives.

Read Snapshot "That Would Be Terrible!" before Question 5

Question Five In 1 Thessalonians 2:4 the apostle Paul says, "We speak as men approved by God to be entrusted with the gospel. We are not trying to please men but God, who tests our hearts." Paul is saying, "We should be determined to be God-pleasers." Put another way, Paul is saying, "I don't need to check the Nielsen ratings three times a day to get the scoop on how I'm doing with everybody. If I love God with my heart, soul, mind, and strength, and if I'm attempting to serve God and others, I can be sure God is smiling. When God is pleased with me, I really don't need to be all that concerned about those people who might be frowning."

Any time you catch yourself saying, "Oh, that would be terrible" or "What would so-and-so say?" or "That would be a disaster," grab hold of yourself and affirm that you are probably exaggerating how destructive the consequences would actually be. At the root of this is probably the attempt to please all of the people all the time, and God does not expect that of you. Have a private conversation with yourself and refuse to be tyrannized by the pressures of pleasing all the people all the time.

Read Snapshot "I Need This!" before Question 6

Question Six Over the years I have had several opportunities to minister to people in many of the developing countries around the world. When I am in those settings, the spirit of truth invades my soul and shows me the difference between a *need* and a *want*. In times like those I am reminded of the need for us to apologize to God for all the things we call needs when in actuality they are wants.

This does not mean we should never bring our needs to God. The truth is, in His grace, our loving God has plenty of room for supplying our needs and often our wants. Just because something is a want does not make it wrong or bad, but we need to be honest before God and acknowledge the difference.

When you hear yourself saying "I need that," let the bells, whistles, and sirens go off. Say to yourself, "Wait a minute. That is not a need, it is a want."

Read Snapshot "God Will Never Forgive You for That!" before Question 7

Question Seven In Revelation 12:10 Satan is called the accuser. His preferred strategy is to point the piercing finger of accusation and to whisper accusing lies in our ears until we believe one of the Devil's lies. Usually, after we believe a lie of the Devil's, we fall into spiritual despair. The "God will never forgive you" lie needs to be exposed and driven out of our thinking.

There are five verses I believe every believer should memorize if they want to be armed to fight against this lie. These verses are:

> "Come now, let us reason together," says the LORD. "Though your sins are like scarlet, they shall be as white as snow; though they are red as crimson, they shall be like wool."
>
> *Isaiah 1:18*

> " ... For I will forgive their wickedness and will remember their sins no more."
>
> *Jeremiah 31:34*

> " ... as far as the east is from the west, so far has he removed our transgressions from us."
>
> *Psalm 103:12*

> "In him we have redemption through his blood, the forgiveness of sins, in accordance with the riches of God's grace ..."
>
> *Ephesians 1:7*

> "If we confess our sins, he is faithful and just and will forgive us our sins and purify us from all unrighteousness."
>
> *1 John 1:9*

I am convinced that every believer should memorize these verses cold. They should be on the tip of our tongue. It's only a matter of time before the best of Christians are going to stub their toes or even to take a swan dive in the pool of sin. When this happens, the accuser is going to start whispering, "God will never forgive you for that." And unless we talk to ourselves and go to war in those conversations, we might just end up believing the lie and being spiritually paralyzed.

Say to yourself, "You're telling me a lie. I know your strategy. God has divine amnesia when it comes to my sins. All my sins have been removed as far as the east is from the west. I've been forgiven according to the riches of God's grace, and I'm not going to believe your lies anymore. I have admitted the sin, and I have accepted the forgiveness that comes through Jesus Christ. You cannot immobilize me by telling me your lies!"

PUTTING YOURSELF IN THE PICTURE

Challenge group members to take time in the coming week to use part or all of this application section as an opportunity for continued growth.

TRUTH OR CONSEQUENCES
EPHESIANS 4:14—16, 25

INTRODUCTION

We all yearn for relationships in which we can be completely honest, open, and vulnerable; in which we can share failures as well as successes, shortcomings as well as strengths; in which we can reveal doubts and fears and find empathy and confidentiality. These intimate, authentic relationships are exactly what God has in mind for us. He created us for relationships, and He wants us to experience them at their best.

In this session we will face the hard reality that to move to this deep level of community in relationships we need to enter "the tunnel of chaos." This is another way of saying we have to learn to tell the truth in our relationships if we want to move from the "safe zone" of pseudocommunity. This truth-telling might mean the compromise of peace for a time, but it will lead to deeper and healthier relationships that will be more than we have ever dreamed of experiencing.

THE BIG PICTURE

Take time to read this introduction with the group. There are suggestions for how this can be done in the beginning of the leader's section.

A WIDE ANGLE VIEW

Question One Years ago I saw a television show where a camera was hidden in a restaurant. An actor entered, sat next to a man eating at the counter, and without saying a word, grabbed some French fries off the man's plate. This scenario was repeated numerous times and, nine times out of ten, the victims never said a word. You knew they were doing a slow burn inside; they clenched their fists and glared at the thief in disbelief. But they never said a word.

When people submerge their true feelings in order to preserve harmony, they undermine the integrity of a relationship.

While there is peace on the surface, underneath there are hurt feelings, troubling questions, and hidden hostilities just waiting to erupt. This is a costly price to pay for a cheap peace, and it inevitably leads to inauthentic relationships.

A BIBLICAL PORTRAIT

Read Ephesians 4:14–16, 25

Questions Two & Three God's plan for His people is to live in real community. A vital prerequisite for this is truth-telling. When we play it safe by keeping the peace at all costs, we compromise the possibility of building real community.

This passage gives the image of a physical body as a comparison to how we relate with other followers of Christ. The apostle Paul says that if we want health in our relationships, we need to get rid of falsehood and start telling the truth. It sounds so simple. But, so often, we fail to do it! Take time as a group to discuss the values of telling the truth, even when telling the truth might thrust chaos into the relationship temporarily. Also, take time to identify some of the common falsehoods that exist in various areas of life. If we are going to be habitual truth-tellers, we need to identify where falsehood is lurking and learn how to drive it out of our lives.

SHARPENING THE FOCUS

Read Snapshot "Peacekeeping vs. Truth-Telling" before Question 4

Questions Four & Five Scott Peck, in his book entitled *The Different Drum*, presents an interesting theory about relationships. He emphasizes that God created human beings to be in what he calls "communal relationships"; that is, relationships that are honest, truthful, supportive, open, tender, accountable, and trusting. He says we are designed by God to yearn for those kinds of relationships. He also says, "Because we all tend to choose peacekeeping over truth-telling, most of us don't ever really experience the kind of true communal relationships God wants for us." Instead, most of us end up settling for what he calls "pseudocommunal relationships." Peck describes pseudocommunal relationships as those that are basically surface level and safe. Failures aren't shared. Hurt feelings are covered up. Frustrations aren't aired. Difficult probing questions aren't asked or answered. The underlying rule in pseudo-communal relationships is, "Don't disturb the peace!"

Read Snapshot "Pseudocommunity" before Question 6

Questions Six & Seven Pseudocommunal relationships tend to deteriorate over time. Both parties start carrying around secret agendas which aren't being discussed. Both parties start feeling a little misunderstood, offended, and put off. They feel taken for granted and unappreciated. Then detachment sets in. Distrust and bitterness escalate, and the relationship dies from the inside out. Sadly, this describes many marriages, friendships, and family relationships.

As your group begins to draw a picture of what pseudocommunal relationships look like, they will probably begin to recognize some of their own relationships in this picture. Invite group members to identify one specific relationship they have that bears the marks of pseudocommunity. Encourage them to communicate what is standing in the way of truth-telling in this relationship. This will help prepare them for the challenging process of entering the tunnel of chaos.

Read Snapshot "The Tunnel of Chaos" before Question 8

Questions Eight & Nine My wife and I learned about pseudocommunity and the tunnel of chaos the hard way. Our story might help your group identify some of the risks and benefits of entering the tunnel of chaos.

During a vacation at a beautiful lake in Wisconsin, I asked Lynne to join me on the dock. It was a lovely evening; the water shimmered in the golden glow of the sinking sun. It was the perfect time for a little "heart-to-heart." I carefully articulated the truth as I saw it. My communication skills left a bit to be desired, but I spoke as lovingly and sensitively as I knew how to at that time. I fully expected a comfortable conversation and a heartfelt apology.

Instead I watched as my beautiful, spiritual, well-mannered, five-foot-four, one-hundred-and-five-pound French poodle turned into a Doberman pinscher. With both ears laid back, her eyes on fire, and her teeth bared, she let me have it! I couldn't believe it. I decided then and there that truth-telling was a bad idea. Maybe pseudocommunity wasn't ideal, but it sure beat chaos. I wanted my French poodle back! I decided to opt for Plan B. Submerge the feelings. Suppress the truth. Ignore the issues. Back off. Keep the peace.

In all fairness to Lynne, I have to tell you that her attempts at truth-telling had met with the same resistance. More than once in the early years of our marriage, she tried to tell me how deeply my workaholism was wounding her. More than once, I stonewalled her. I suggested that she fix her insecurities, grow up, and "help me instead of hold me back."

Eventually she too settled for the easy way out. What did we accomplish? We simply postponed our appointment in the tunnel. We thought that if we ignored our problems they would eventually go away. Instead they turned over and over in our minds, like meat on a rotisserie grill, and became more and more inflamed. The chaos we eventually faced made the evening on the dock look like child's play.

We made the mistake of believing that the other's initial defensiveness was the end of the world, so we backed off. In reality, the defensive reaction was simply the opening to the tunnel of chaos. If we had entered the tunnel and then talked our problems through to a resolution, we could have moved into true community. But we were so frightened that we made a U-turn and headed back into years of pseudocommunity.

Thank God, our frustration eventually led us to tell the truth. We did find out that the tunnel of chaos is a frightening place to be. But when we came out the other side, we realized that going through the tunnel was a small price to pay for the open communication and freed-up love of an authentic relationship.

PUTTING YOURSELF IN THE PICTURE

Challenge group members to take time in the coming week to use part or all of this application section as an opportunity for continued growth.

GAMES PEOPLE PLAY
JOHN 4:7–26

INTRODUCTION

In this session we will look at three of the common shortcuts people take to avoid the tunnel of chaos. The problem is that all of these shortcuts are really dead ends. In the introduction to the session there are five examples of games people play to avoid entering the tunnel of chaos. This list is certainly not exhaustive. However, in this lesson we will focus on three of the most common styles of communication we use in an effort to avoid coming out and speaking the truth. The goal of this session is to help group members identify where these unhealthy patterns exist in their relationships and to learn how to begin communicating with honesty and authenticity.

Note: As a group leader it is important to communicate that these characters could be male or female, young or old, single or married. The fact of the matter is, each of us can see ourselves in all of the characters if we look hard enough.

THE BIG PICTURE

Take time to read this introduction with the group. There are suggestions for how this can be done in the beginning of the leader's section.

A BIBLICAL PORTRAIT

Read John 4:7–26

Questions Two & Three The Bible has communicated the same message for a couple of thousand years now: Don't build relationships on pretense. Don't let the sun go down on disturbances and frustrations in a relationship. Stop lying to each other. Tell each other the truth. Relationships that are going to last won't be built in any other way.

Jesus knew we would be tempted to play games and try to take shortcuts in our communication. He knew that human beings often prefer peacekeeping to truth-telling. Knowing this, Jesus modeled what it meant to speak the truth with clarity and confidence . . . even when it was hard to do. In this encounter with the woman at the well, Jesus gives a powerful example of truth-telling on many levels. Take time as a group to reflect on the example of Jesus and discuss the various ways He told the truth.

SHARPENING THE FOCUS

Read Snapshot "Henry the Hint-Dropper" before Question 4

Questions Four & Five Have you ever played the hint-dropping game? People who play this game think they are being so clever. The person on the receiving end of all the hints knows what's going on, but usually refuses to respond out of sheer rebellion toward the technique being used. After a time, however, the person on the receiving end of all the hints usually blurts out, "Look, if you've got a problem, let's talk about it. If you've got an issue, let's put it on the table. Enough cute stuff. No more games!"

What happens then? It puts the relationship smack-dab in the middle of the tunnel of chaos, which is precisely what Henry the Hint-Dropper was trying to avoid all along. Hint-dropping only bogs down attempts at moving toward community. It simply postpones the inevitable appointment at the truth-telling tunnel. The damage done to a relationship during the hint-dropping process can be very serious. We need to commit ourselves to speak the truth in love.

Read Snapshot "Mary the Manipulator" before Question 6

Questions Six & Seven Mary the Manipulator thinks she is going to reshape Carl into somebody with whom she can finally experience true community. Little does she know what's going on in Carl's head. Carl knows a game is being played. He's lying in his natural habitat, his couch, marveling at Mary's arrogance. He is amazed at her moralizing. He is astounded at her not-so-well-concealed attempts to control him.

Over time, given enough "shoulds" and "oughts," this mild-mannered man is going to come to life. He's going to stand up to Mary some day and say, "Enough is enough. Who in the world do you think you are? God made me different from you, Mary. I'm not better or worse; I'm just different. Who made you the standard by which I, or anybody else, should be judged? If you would like me to take some night classes or take up jogging, say it straight. God is the only One who tells me what I should and shouldn't do. You can tell me what you would *like* to have me do or not do. Got it, Mary?"

What's happening when this mild-mannered man stands up to Mary? They are entering that tunnel of chaos, the very place Mary didn't want to go through. Manipulation does not work. You can play all the games you want to play, but in the end you will find yourself having to go through the very tunnel you were trying to avoid. Are you tired of being manipulated? Then get yourself in a position where you can say, "Don't 'should' me or 'ought' me. If you would like me to do something, then just say so. But don't try to recreate me or manipulate me. I'm not going to play those games."

Read Snapshot "Gary the Guilt-Tripper" before Question 8

Questions Eight & Nine I've never met a person who responded well to having a guilt-trip placed on them. It just seems to bring out the worst in all of us. But some people just keep trying to use this shortcut in an effort to avoid the tunnel of chaos. The problem is it never leads to real community. Allow group members time to honestly evaluate the presence of this tactic in their relationships and the cost of this approach to communication.

PUTTING YOURSELF IN THE PICTURE

Challenge group members to take time in the coming week to use part or all of this application section as an opportunity for continued growth.

Expressing Positive Emotions

Luke 17:11—19

Introduction

The importance of giving and receiving positive truthful expressions cannot be overemphasized. This is why the Bible states so clearly in 1 Thessalonians 5:11, "Encourage one another and build each other up." In Hebrews 3:13 we read, "Encourage one another daily, as long as it is called Today, so that none of you may be hardened by sin's deceitfulness."

After the past few sessions, it might seem that expressing positive emotions would be easy to do. But just as telling the truth in tough situations is not always something we do naturally, expressing positive emotions is also a learned skill. There are many excuses for why we don't express positive emotions. Sometimes we say, "I just don't know how to express myself that way. We didn't do that in our home as I was growing up as a child." Others say, "I have positive feelings toward other people, but I don't consider myself to be the articulate type. I just don't know what to say." Still others are genuinely afraid that if they express positive feelings, the person they affirm will get a big head and become an overnight egotist. In this session we are going to try and move past these roadblocks and develop some skills for expressing positive emotions.

The Big Picture

Take time to read this introduction with the group. There are suggestions for how this can be done in the beginning of the leader's section.

A BIBLICAL PORTRAIT

Read Luke 17:11–19

Questions Two & Three For many years I made a serious mistake in my prayers of thanksgiving to God. I would catalog all of the blessings God had brought into my life silently in my mind. As I reflected on all God had done for me, I would experience a fullness of His blessing on my life. I made the mistake of saying to myself that *feeling* this great fullness in my heart was the same as *expressing* my feelings of thanksgiving.

When I came to understand the difference between feeling gratitude and expressing thanksgiving, it marked a changing point in the way I pray. Now I make it a point to *express* thanksgiving to God. I break it down very specifically. I thank God for answered prayer, spiritual blessings, relational blessings, material blessings, and anything else that comes to my mind. Sometimes I speak it, other times I write it—there are even times that I sing it! The key is that I am committed to openly express my thankfulness to God. I can tell a big difference in my prayers, and I know God is pleased with the expression of my thanksgiving to Him.

Some years ago I studied the episode in the life of Jesus when the ten dying lepers petition Jesus to heal them. Jesus says to them, "Now, you can leave My presence and by faith go show yourselves to the priests." While they were traveling, they were all miraculously healed. As I was studying that passage, I asked myself, "I wonder what those ten lepers felt the moment they were miraculously healed from their terminal illness?" Certainly, the first thing that came to my mind was that all ten must have had great feelings of gratitude and thankfulness towards Jesus; they must have all felt an internal sense of appreciation and joy.

What strikes me about the story is that only one of the lepers made a U-turn. He went all the way back to Jesus, bowed down, and expressed his feelings of thanksgiving to Him. This expression of feelings made a difference to Jesus. If you read the text carefully, you can see Jesus showing His vulnerability. He asked, "Where are the other nine fellows?" If you read between the lines, it's as though Jesus is saying, "You mean, they are just out there feeling grateful, thankful, and joyous, but they didn't come back and express it? I wish they would have expressed it to Me." Expressing positive emotions mattered to Jesus and it should matter to us!

Sharpening the Focus

Read Snapshot "A Look" before Question 4

Questions Four & Five One of the snapshots I carry around in the permanent file of my mind is a look from my dad. Those who have lost mothers and fathers already know how important snapshots and memories can be. My dad wasn't all that much of a verbal person, but oh, he could communicate a lot in a look.

I was just an elementary school-age kid when my dad taught me how to dock his sailboat. We'd go out sailing on Lake Michigan and come back in the river and head towards the dock. And then we had to put that long sailboat in a narrow slip. To a young boy, the slip looked narrower than the boat! In docking the boat we would have to take into consideration the current of the river, the velocity and the direction of the wind, the speed of the approach, and then put the boat in reverse at just the right moment to make sure we would not slam into the dock. Over time my father patiently taught me the ins and outs of how to dock a boat.

Then the day came when he stood up on the foredeck and said, "Billy, it's all yours." I can remember doing all those calculations, looking at the river, trying to sense the wind, looking at the wind teller on the shroud, and inching the boat forward. I remember doing the best I could to bring that sailboat straight into the slip and having it stop just right. My dad, whose back was turned to me, looked over his shoulder and gave me one of those "Not bad for a little guy . . . I'm proud of you" looks! That moment, that look of love, is a snapshot I carry with me everywhere I go.

We need to learn the importance and power of a look. It can burn a memory of pain into someone's heart or a memory of love and affirmation. Sadly, there are too many husbands and wives and kids who do not have these snapshots of looks of love in their memory banks.

How about it? Are you ready to give a look of love and affirmation? It can happen in the home, with children, with friends, or with coworkers. Just a nod of approval across the department at the office. A smile. A look of love. Powerful!

Read Snapshot "A Word" before Question 6

Questions Six & Seven A department head on our church staff said, "Someone wrote me a note recently that said, 'God is using you in a powerful way. The sky is the limit as to what

God can do through you in the future.'" That staff member said, "When I read, 'the sky is the limit for me,' it just made my heart leap."

A friend told me about the night his wife said, "Of all the women in the world you could marry, I want to thank you for choosing me." Those words of truth did not have to be said, but when they were, what a powerful expression of love and affirmation!

One Monday morning, one of our church members and a leader who I respect greatly, called me. During the conversation he said, "Recently, in one of your messages, you made a point with such clarity and power that I wanted to stand up where I was sitting in the balcony and cheer. I was so proud of you." Those two sentences impacted me more than I can express.

How important are constructive words? What do they do to needy souls? How do they impact beaten down lives? They are like a fountain of life. They supply new energy, new resources. The power of spoken, positive, truthful words is amazing!

Read Snapshot "A Touch" before Question 8

Questions Eight & Nine Some time ago one of our staff members was talking about his experiences of affirmation in the home where he had grown up with eleven siblings. He said, "On Friday nights, all of us would pile into our station wagon and we would go out to eat." He continued, "You have to understand that, with twelve kids, it was a real honor to cycle through and end up being able to sit in the front seat between Mom and Dad. I mean, that was really special." I did the math and realized that with twelve children, you sat between Mom and Dad four times a year. So it *was* very special. This particular staff member said, "You know, one time I can remember my turn coming and I got to sit between Mom and Dad. On the way to the restaurant, my mother just put her hand on my knee and just kept rubbing it a little bit." He said, "I've never forgotten that." It was a touch of love.

A person's touch has the power to communicate love and care like few other things can. Consider this story. During the first day of an introductory speech class, the teacher was going around the room having students introduce themselves. Each student was to respond to two questions: (1) What do I like about myself? and (2) What don't I like about myself? Nearly hiding in the back of the room was Dorothy. Her long, red hair hung down around her face, almost obscuring it from view. When it was Dorothy's turn to introduce herself, there was silence in the room. Thinking, perhaps, that she had not heard the question, the teacher moved his chair over near her and gently repeated the question. Again, there was only silence. Finally, with a deep sigh, Dorothy sat up in her chair and she pulled back her hair. Covering nearly all of one side of her face was a large, irregularly shaped birthmark, nearly as red as her hair. "That," she said, "should show you what I don't like about myself." Moved with compassion, the professor leaned over and gave her a hug. He said, "It's okay, honey. I think you're beautiful and so does God." Dorothy cried uncontrollably for almost twenty minutes. Soon, the other students had gathered around her and were offering her comfort as well. When she finally could talk, she dabbed the tears from her eyes and said to the professor, "I have wanted for someone to hug me and say those words my whole life. Why couldn't my parents have done that? My mother has never touched my face."

PUTTING YOURSELF IN THE PICTURE

Challenge group members to take time in the coming week to use part or all of this application section as an opportunity for continued growth.

HEARING THE TRUTH

JAMES 1:19—20

INTRODUCTION

In this final session in our series, I want to focus in on the challenge of learning how to *receive* truthful words from other people. When someone summons the courage to tell us the truth, we need to be ready to hear it. First, we will look at the challenge of receiving and responding to the hard words other people speak to us. We have to learn to overcome our natural human instincts in order to receive the hard truth from others. It takes a ton of courage, self-control, and maturity. In this session we will also look at how to hear the truth when others speak words of affirmation and encouragement. This is also difficult for many people.

THE BIG PICTURE

Take time to read this introduction with the group. There are suggestions for how this can be done in the beginning of the leader's section.

A WIDE ANGLE VIEW

Question One What goes through your mind when someone says, "Do you want the truth, or should I lie and make you feel good?" Have you ever heard words like, "Honey, how do you like my tie?" and you are faced with telling that person the truth or settling for a lie that would make the person feel good. There's something in each of us that wants to say, "I'll take the lie. Make me feel good. I would just as soon feel good than feel bad any day." Then there's another part of us that says, "Go ahead. Tell me the truth even if it hurts."

A BIBLICAL PORTRAIT

Read James 1:19–20

Question Two If I were to paraphrase this passage, I would put it this way: "My friends, be quick to hear. Listen even when others are speaking hard words. Be slow to react. Be very slow to anger and retaliation. For the anger of man will never achieve the righteousness of God."

Our goal is to convert the energy once used for denial, retaliation, and rationalizing into listening power. This requires self-control and courage. We need to hear others, contemplate what they say, become vulnerable, and reflect on what we hear. We all need to learn how to "be quick to hear, slow to speak, slow to anger." We need to realize that there might be truth in what this person is saying, and that it might make a contribution to our life.

SHARPENING THE FOCUS

Read Snapshot "Hearing the Truth, Even When It Hurts" before Question 3

Question Three The vast majority of us tend to respond reflexively and instinctively to the hard-to-hear truthful words that fly at us from other people. Almost before the other person finishes his conversation, our minds are racing to figure out ways to protect our fragile feelings. Without listening or reflecting on the content of what is being communicated, we fire up our defensive weapons—the weapons of denial, retaliation, and rationalization. Instead, we need to be ready to hear the truth, and this means dropping our natural defenses.

Questions Four & Five We all have a defense network that protects us from the hurt that comes from others. We need to identify what specific patterns we see in our lives and commit ourselves to not following these same patterns every time someone wants to speak the truth to us. In this session we are focusing on three specific patterns that are very common: denial, retaliation, and rationalization.

Take time as a group to clarify what you feel is the best antidote for each of these response patterns. There is no right and wrong answer here as much as the need to identify ways to resist these patterns.

One possible antidote to denial is confession. When someone speaks the hard truth to us and we realize they are right, we need to admit where we have wronged them. This act of confession destroys the possibility for denial. When we admit our guilt, we battle the tendency to defend ourselves with the weapons of denial.

Seeking peace is one antidote to retaliation. Jesus talks about being peacemakers. Instead of clenching fists and getting ready for a fight, we need to commit ourselves to extending a hand and seeking peace.

When people speak the hard truth to us, we can easily begin rationalizing and explaining away our actions or attitudes. In an effort to battle this tendency, we need to measure ourselves by the unchanging standard of God's Word, the Bible. If we measure ourselves by our own standards, we can rationalize almost anything. However, when we set our lives up against the solid and unchanging standard of God's truth, rationalization no longer works. We see our actions, attitudes, words, and thoughts in a whole new light and can't explain them away.

Read Snapshot "Hearing the Truth, Even When It Feels Good!" before Question 6

Questions Six, Seven, & Eight When we refuse Spirit-led, well-intentioned affirmations from other people, we tend to extinguish their enthusiasm for affirming us and other people. When somebody affirms or encourages you, why not simply respond by saying, "Thank you for saying that. I appreciate your words." Or say, "Thanks. You made my day." Sometimes, as I'm affirming my daughter, she'll say, "I'll give you twenty minutes to stop that, Dad." Those kinds of responses tend to encourage the affirmer. And we all know that the world would be a better place if there was a lot more encouragement and affirmation.

Read Snapshot "Hearing the Truth from God" before Question 9

Question Nine This is a great opportunity for group members to tell some of their stories of faith. If time allows, have one or two group members tell about when they became a follower of Christ and how their life has been impacted by this decision.

Question Ten There might be a person in your group who needs to make a decision to hear the truth of God today. They may need to bow their head and say, "Lord, I want to stop playing games. I've been suppressing the truth. I want to confess my sinfulness and ask for Jesus Christ to forgive me for my sins. I want to trust Him and begin a relationship with Him right now. I don't need religion, but I do need to know the risen Savior."

If someone is at this point in his life, take time as a group to pray with him. Others might seek you out after the group is over. Make yourself available and be ready to invite them to pray and ask for God to extend them forgiveness through Jesus Christ.

PUTTING YOURSELF IN THE PICTURE

Challenge group members to take time in the coming week to use part or all of this application section as an opportunity for continued growth.

ADDITIONAL WILLOW CREEK RESOURCES

Small Group Resources

Coaching Life-Changing Small Group Leaders, by Bill Donahue and Greg Bowman
The Complete Book of Questions, by Garry Poole
The Connecting Church, by Randy Frazee
Leading Life-Changing Small Groups, by Bill Donahue and the Willow Creek Team
The Seven Deadly Sins of Small Group Ministry, by Bill Donahue and Russ Robinson
Walking the Small Group Tightrope, by Bill Donahue and Russ Robinson

Evangelism Resources

Becoming a Contagious Christian (book), by Bill Hybels and Mark Mittelberg
The Case for a Creator, by Lee Strobel
The Case for Christ, by Lee Strobel
The Case for Faith, by Lee Strobel
Seeker Small Groups, by Garry Poole
The Three Habits of Highly Contagious Christians, by Garry Poole

Spiritual Gifts and Ministry

Network Revised (training course), by Bruce Bugbee and Don Cousins
The Volunteer Revolution, by Bill Hybels
What You Do Best in the Body of Christ—Revised, by Bruce Bugbee

Marriage and Parenting

Fit to Be Tied, by Bill and Lynne Hybels
Surviving a Spiritual Mismatch in Marriage, by Lee and Leslie Strobel

Ministry Resources

An Hour on Sunday, by Nancy Beach
Building a Church of Small Groups, by Bill Donahue and Russ Robinson
The Heart of the Artist, by Rory Noland
Making Your Children's Ministry the Best Hour of Every Kid's Week, by Sue Miller and David Staal
Thriving as an Artist in the Church, by Rory Noland

Curriculum

An Ordinary Day with Jesus, by John Ortberg and Ruth Haley Barton
Becoming a Contagious Christian (kit), by Mark Mittelberg, Lee Strobel, and Bill Hybels
Good Sense Budget Course, by Dick Towner, John Tofilon, and the Willow Creek Team
If You Want to Walk on Water, You've Got to Get Out of the Boat, by John Ortberg with Stephen and Amanda Sorenson
The Life You've Always Wanted, by John Ortberg with Stephen and Amanda Sorenson
The Old Testament Challenge, by John Ortberg with Kevin and Sherry Harney, Mindy Caliguire, and Judson Poling

Willow Creek Association
Vision, Training, Resources for Prevailing Churches

This resource was created to serve you and to help you build a local church that prevails. It is just one of many ministry tools that are part of the Willow Creek Resources® line, published by the Willow Creek Association together with Zondervan.

The Willow Creek Association (WCA) was created in 1992 to serve a rapidly growing number of churches from across the denominational spectrum that are committed to helping unchurched people become fully devoted followers of Christ. Membership in the WCA now numbers over 10,500 Member Churches worldwide from more than ninety denominations.

The Willow Creek Association links like-minded Christian leaders with each other and with strategic vision, training, and resources in order to help them build prevailing churches designed to reach their redemptive potential. Here are some of the ways the WCA does that.

- **A2: Building Prevailing Acts 2 Churches—Today**—an annual two-and-a-half day event, held at Willow Creek Community Church in South Barrington, Illinois, to explore strategies for building churches that reach out to seekers and build believers, and to discover new innovations and breakthroughs from Acts 2 churches around the country.

- **The Leadership Summit**—a once a year, two-and-a-half-day conference to envision and equip Christians with leadership gifts and responsibilities. Presented live at Willow Creek as well as via satellite broadcast to over one hundred locations across North America, this event is designed to increase the leadership effectiveness of pastors, ministry staff, volunteer church leaders, and Christians in the marketplace.

- **Ministry-Specific Conferences**—throughout each year the WCA hosts a variety of conferences and training events—both at Willow Creek's main campus and offsite, across the U.S., and around the world—targeting church leaders and volunteers in ministry-specific areas such as: evangelism, small groups, preaching and teaching, the arts, children, students, women, volunteers, stewardship, raising up resources, etc.

- **Willow Creek Resources®**—provides churches with trusted and field-tested ministry resources in such areas as leadership, evangelism, spiritual formation, spiritual gifts, small groups, stewardship, student ministry, children's ministry, the use of the arts-drama, media, contemporary music —and more.

- **WCA Member Benefits**—includes substantial discounts to WCA training events, a 20 percent discount on all Willow Creek Resources®, *Defining Moments* monthly audio journal for leaders, quarterly *Willow* magazine, access to a Members-Only section on WillowNet, monthly communications, and more. Member Churches also receive special discounts and premier services through WCA's growing number of ministry partners—Select Service Providers—and save an average of $500 annually depending on the level of engagement.

For specific information about WCA conferences, resources, membership, and other ministry services contact:

Willow Creek Association
P.O. Box 3188
Barrington, IL 60011-3188
Phone: 847-570-9812
Fax: 847-765-5046
www.willowcreek.com

Continue building your new community!
New Community Series
BILL HYBELS AND JOHN ORTBERG
with Kevin and Sherry Harney

Exodus: *Journey Toward God* 0-310-22771-2

Parables: *Imagine Life God's Way* 0-310-22881-6

Sermon on the Mount¹: *Connect with God* 0-310-22884-0

Sermon on the Mount²: *Connect with Others* 0-310-22883-2

Acts: *Build Community* 0-310-22770-4

Romans: *Find Freedom* 0-310-22765-8

Philippians: *Run the Race* 0-310-22766-6

Colossians: *Discover the New You* 0-310-22769-0

James: *Live Wisely* 0-310-22767-4

1 Peter: *Stand Strong* 0-310-22773-9

1 John: *Love Each Other* 0-310-22768-2

Revelation: *Experience God's Power* 0-310-22882-4

Look for New Community at your local Christian bookstore.

Continue the Transformation
Pursuing Spiritual Transformation
JOHN ORTBERG, LAURIE PEDERSON,
AND JUDSON POLING

Grace: *An Invitation to a Way of Life* 0-310-22074-2

Growth: *Training vs. Trying* 0-310-22075-0

Groups: *The Life-Giving Power of Community* 0-310-22076-9

Gifts: *The Joy of Serving God* 0-310-22077-7

Giving: *Unlocking the Heart of Good Stewardship* 0-310-22078-5

Fully Devoted: *Living Each Day in Jesus' Name* 0-310-22073-4

Look for Pursuing Spiritual Transformation at your local Christian bookstore.

TOUGH QUESTIONS
Garry Poole and Judson Poling

Softcover

REALITY CHECK SERIES
by Mark Ashton

Everybody's Normal Till You Get to Know Them

John Ortberg

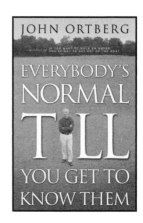

Not you, that's for sure! No one you've ever met, either. None of us are normal according to God's definition, and the closer we get to each other, the plainer that becomes.

Yet for all our quirks, sins, and jagged edges, we need each other. Community is more than just a word—it is one of our most fundamental requirements. So how do flawed, abnormal people such as ourselves master the forces that can drive us apart and come together in the life-changing relationships God designed us for?

In *Everybody's Normal Till You Get to Know Them*, teacher and bestselling author John Ortberg zooms in on the things that make community tick. You'll get a thought-provoking look at God's heart, at others, and at yourself. Even better, you'll gain wisdom and tools for drawing closer to others in powerful, impactful ways. With humor, insight, and a gift for storytelling, Ortberg shows how community pays tremendous dividends in happiness, health, support, and growth. It's where all of us weird, unwieldy people encounter God's love in tangible ways and discover the transforming power of being loved, accepted, and valued just the way we are.

Softcover: 0-310-23927-3
Unabridged Audio Pages® CD: 0-310-25083-8
Unabridged Audio Pages® Cassette: 0-310-25082-X

GRAND RAPIDS, MICHIGAN 49530 USA

WWW.ZONDERVAN.COM

We want to hear from you. Please send your comments about this book to us in care of zreview@zondervan.com. Thank you.

GRAND RAPIDS, MICHIGAN 49530 USA
WWW.ZONDERVAN.COM